UNSCREWED

An outline for saving (Collectively) "our" ass, our family and our country!

LEONARD MARSHALL

First Amendment Free Press®
New York - New York

Acknowledgements

My life is the sum of all the people I've known throughout my 65 years. I have always thought that I lived an "average" or "normal" life, but I was wrong. I have lived, and continue to live an amazing life due to all of them.

I have to start with my mom, Frances Harriet Marshall, who brought me into this world in a Blizzard and has stuck with me ever since.

To my Dad, Irving, whom everyone loved and adored and left us way too soon.

To both pairs of Grandparents, Dorothy and Edward Brock, and Esther and Benjamin Marshall.

To my Uncles Phil and Norman and Aunt Marilyn who survived living with Irving, and their spouses, Norma, Naomi and Big Lenny, who all became family despite Irving.

To my Aunt Roberta who baby-sat me while she was trying to date my soon to be Uncle Mike. Belated apologies to both.

Most of all, to my companion and wife for 20 years, Robin Price-Marshall. Without her, I would have never survived.

This Booklet is Dedicated to all the people of the last 250 years, who worked, fought and died for this Country.
May we honor their memories by working and sacrificing today, as much has been sacrificed in the past.

First Amendment Free Press®
New York - New York

Table of Contents

Really?
About as useful as the Department
of Education.

UNSCREWED

An outline for saving (Collectively) "our" Ass, our Family and our Country!

If you aren't scared to death about the future of this country, you must already be dead. For the rest of us, hang on tight and let's get to saving our collective backsides.

This outline is current as of December 7th (Another Day of Infamy), after the 2016 Presidential election between the 2 worst candidates in recent U.S. history. Don't be distracted by the daily lies, distortions and mudslinging, it's all there to distract you and keep you from doing anything about it. Keeping everybody all stirred up so that the politicians and their OWNERS can keep stealing, cheating and robbing from the rest of us. The Constitution proclaims that "Freedom of the Press" which in today's world equals all the media, "may not be abridged", but what about the "Freedom of the People" to whom the media lies to every day?

Today, "Media" is everything that we see and hear, and just because it comes over the "Social" media and is beamed directly to you doesn't mean it's true. It's now ALL hearsay and none of it can be trusted. What you can trust, is that its purpose is to influence you. Even bald- faced blatant lies have an effect even when you KNOW they're lies. It's human nature and these information charlatans know it, right down to the last decimal point and dollar sign.

"*WE THE PEOPLE*" The most abused, misused and misunderstood slogan in the history of the United States. Used by the wealthy, white male landowners to drum up support against Great Britain. A great slogan in a campaign to steal the land from the Crown and to set up their own little fiefdoms here on this continent.

Thankfully, they succeeded and this country was born. But to keep what they had taken, they had to share it with others, who like themselves, were more interested in their own welfare, and again, thankfully so. It resulted in the compromise we call the Constitution and literally out of thin air, produced a new type of country, heretofore never seen before on Earth..

Franklin said in answering the question of what have we conceived, replied; "A republic, if you can keep it".

You must understand, we are an experiment, we are not destined to continue forever, and we can most certainly fail. History and current affairs seem to be leaning heavily towards failure, something that we must not allow to happen. Despite what we are experiencing, we can take steps to correct our problems and rebuild and strengthen our country. We must take on the role of leaders, not followers, not just voters. Voting for someone that you wouldn't trust with your dog, is NOT the way. We all must get involved, and believe it or not, we have found the way to do just that.

Most people have never even heard about **ARTICLE THE FIRST**, the real First Amendment to the Constitution. Despite everything that you are going to hear about it, it WAS ratified and is actually the law of the land. The history of the Constitution and what is commonly called "The Bill of Rights" that you may or may not have been taught is wrong, and the mistakes have only multiplied across the last 200 years. But never mind that for a moment.

What is needed now is concerned, involved leadership and "Article the First" gives it back to us, "We The People". It simply states that at this stage of our Country's size and population that we are supposed to have 1 congressman for every 50,000 people, 15 times the number we now have. Imagine having a congressman in your backyard, instead of a big-wig having a congressman in his back pocket.

Imagine yourself being able to run for office without having to raise millions of dollars and making millions of promises to people who only want to own you. Or if you don't want to run for office, consider being able to look over the shoulder of your representative and influencing him to do the right thing for you, your family, your town, your city, your state, and your country. If you believe in our Constitution and honor and love our country, help convince OUR government to follow and observe the RATIFIED LAWS OF THE LAND. Bring responsive and responsible governance back. The only place to fix the system is by taking control of Congress. It is the key to fixing the whole rotten mess in DC, it holds the purse-strings, the power to tax, the absolute power over the Supreme court, and can properly control the Presidency, which has usurped both Congress and the Court.

"WE THE PEOPLE" can and MUST control the Congress, and "**ARTICLE THE FIRST**" may be the last alternative to the *Ball and Musket* that we still have.

Here's a short Civics lesson, (the long one comes later).

Three Quick Definitions:

Democracy: The belief in freedom and equality between people, or a system of government based on this belief, in which power is either held by elected representatives or directly by the people themselves.

Republic: A state in which supreme power is held by the people and their elected representatives, and which has an elected or nominated president rather than a monarch.

Tyranny: government by a ruler or small group of people who have unlimited power over the people…

We were designed to be a unique Democratic Republic. Our government is only *Allowed* to **govern**, only with the *Consent* of the *governed*. The Founders knew that the odds for success were very small, in the entire history of the world, we were the first to attempt it on a large scale. They understood that it was going to be a balancing act, from the very beginning, which is why so many seemingly strange and undemocratic compromises were made. Without them, without the blend of patriotism and greed that occurred during that period of time, there would be NO America at all. They gave us the start, they gave us the tools, they gave us everything necessary to build this Nation. It is up to us, all of us, to pick up these tools and get back to work. Their legacy is our duty, and with the 2016 Presidential election now over, now is urgently the time to get busy.

Rights of United States Citizens

- Vote in Federal elections
- Serve on a jury
- Bring family members to the United States
- Obtain citizenship for children born abroad
- Travel with a U.S. passport
- Run for Federal office
- Become eligible for Federal grants and scholarship
- AND *All* the other rights not given to the Federal
-   and State governments.

Responsibilities of U.S. Citizens:

- Support and defend the Constitution
- Serve the country when required
- Participate in the democratic process
- Respect and obey federal, state, and local laws
- Respect the rights, beliefs, and opinions of others
- Participate in your local community

Don't be distracted or fooled by the "OUTRAGE of the Day". They, and the people that try to scare us with these NEWS stories are DESIGNED to distract you from working on and fixing the real, underlying problems. They are used to make money, get votes and boost ratings. Unless you are watching the Weather report, they aren't there to help, and the way the weather is reported, they're not much help either. Reporting by standing out in the middle of a hurricane in Florida or in a Blizzard in North Dakota is just grandstanding for more ratings and hasn't added any value since the advent of "Live" broadcasting since the Eisenhower administration.

There are a number of very important, but basic tasks that must be accomplished to put our nation back on the right track. You can rank them yourself on which you thing is more important, but certain things must be performed in a certain order to have the proper result.

Our Federal government is badly broken and the rot has spread over our nation, down thru our State and Local governments.

The only Constitutional fix is the active institution of **"ARTICLE THE FIRST"**. Congress must be totally changed and restructured first, before any other changes can occur and here's why:

The Federal Legislative branch consists of two branches, the Upper House known as the Senate, and the Lower House known as the House of Representatives. The Executive branch consists of the President and his Cabinet and the Vice-President, who also presides over the Senate. The Judicial branch included the Federal Supreme Court and all lower Federal Courts.

I've put the three branches together because under the Constitution, they are supposed to be equal and are there to balance each other and to take action when things get out of whack. Things are now so out of whack, even the AFLAC duck was forced to call the whole situation "fowl" and quit. It's time for "We the People" to stand up and whack it back into shape.

Fixing Congress can be done due to the very nature of the Institution. Inside the House & Senate exists a very strange place indeed.

While in these Chambers, outside rules and laws don't apply, (Even Gravity has a hard time, judging from the results), they make the rules out of that singularly strange atmosphere that existswith the within that hallowed edifice and change them whenever the political winds change. It has been said that you could shoot a colleague on the House Floor and receive nothing more than a "Censure" vote for excessive noise. The Executive and Judicial branches and other State and Local Governmental agencies could and cannot interfere.

In sharp contrast, the Constitution gives Congress carte-blanche oversight in the powers of the Executive and has the singular power to re-define and restructure the Judicial Branch. It's implicit and explicit in the Constitution.

Here's the Plan

FIRST:

"ARTICLE THE FIRST" must be put into action and enforced. Once that has started, and elections have taken place as per the Constitution, the many members of the House will be able to re-organize themselves and literally build a new design and operational procedures. It will be very disruptive in the short term, (It's meant to be), and will force positive change and the emergence of new representative leaders, unencumbered by the two criminal parties that now run the nation.

Envision 6,600 Congressional offices, 1 in each district, across the land. All available so that *You* can visit, see and talk with *Your* Representative. In an office full of computers with large screens all the way around, giving us a working portrait of our government at work, all directly linked to the House of Representatives where any Bill or government business is immediatly available to ALL members. No more votes on phantom legislation, no more threats that you can't see the Bill until you vote on it! (Thank-You Nancy Pelosi and Harry Reid). Let our Representative leaders write a new "Contract for America", instead of a Contract **ON** America.

SECOND:

And while we are here, let's propose a "Pledge" for all incoming Representatives. (Would be good for Senators, too, but I don't thing that would be politically viable, we're ONLY changing the House).

"Immediately ridding the American Political process of the severely corruptive effects of special interests, now made even worse by the Supreme Court's decision in Citizen's United, is not really complicated at all: There is no reason to give up on America. There is no reason to overreact. There is no reason to change the Constitution. There is no reason to even change the laws. Just change the 'Rules'."

- Eugene Martin LaVergne

Independence Hall
Philadelphia, Pennsylvania
September 15, 2012

Change the Rules Pledge:

I _____,

THE UNDERSIGNED DO HEREBY
[Name of Candidate]

DECLARE AND PLEDGE THIS _____ DAY OF
_____, In the Year of 20__

THE FOLLOWING:

1)   That I am a candidate for the United States Senate or the United States House of Representatives on the November _, 20__ General Election Ballot, and that as a candidate for Congress I hereby voluntarily agree that my campaign organization and committee, and any political action committee I am in any way associated with, will not accept a political donation from any union, from any corporation, or from any other political action committee, political party committee, or candidate committee that has accepted a donation from any union or corporation, and that any donation I may have already received that violates the standards I have now voluntarily agreed to be bound by will be returned to the donor or donated to charity.

2)   That if elected, I hereby pledge that on the following January, 20__, I will immediately propose to the President Pro Tempore of the Senate or the Speaker of the House of Representatives, as the case may be, to immediately amend the Rules to henceforth provide that:

(A) Any Member that has not voluntarily complied with the standards of the "Change the Rules Pledge", shall be specifically excluded from holding any Party Leadership Position, any Chair, Vice-Chair, seat or voting privileges on any Committee or Sub-Committee,

(B) That any such Member shall retain the right to introduce legislation, and to vote on all questions to the Committee of the Whole Senate or the Committee of the Whole House of Representatives, called to be taken by the President Pro Tempore of the Senate or the Speaker of the House of Representatives, as the case may be, and

(C) That any Member who has voluntarily agreed to be bound by the "Change the Rules Pledge" but has nonetheless received indirect union or corporate support in favor of their candidacy with a value of in excess of $1,000, shall be excluded from personally testifying before or voting in Committee or Sub-Committee in favor or against any proposed legislation that will in any way affect the legal status or pecuniary interest of the union or corporation that provided indirect support, unless the Committee or Sub-Committee finds that the indirect support for the candidacy of the Member from the union or corporation was extended in bad faith and for the purpose and design of disqualifying the Member from testifying or voting in Committee or Sub-Committee on legislation on a given issue.

_____

[Signature of Candidate]

_____

[Printed Name of Candidate]

_____

[State and, if applicable, District]

Explanation of Pledge and Background

According to the United States Supreme Court's January 2011 decision in Citizens United v. Federal Election Commission, corporations which are not "persons" eligible to vote but rather are fictitious legal entities created under State Law to insulate a business owner from liability from civil lawsuit, are now entitled to the same right to engage in unregulated political speech under the [First Amendment] as "actual persons". The effect of the Citizens United decision on the American Political process has been swift and dramatic. In the last 19 months corporations have dedicated tens of millions of dollars of shareholder's money to support candidates or oppose candidates seeking election or re-election to Congress. This is the first election for Congress since the Citizens United decision. The decision on which candidates for Congress will receive corporate support or corporate opposition is determined solely based upon financial considerations of which candidate will likely best advance or protect the financial interests or legal status of the corporation. There is a very real concern that the millions of dollars in corporate money will mute if not stifle the political voice and political will of the actual "real people" who populate America.

Opposition to the Supreme Court's opinion in Citizens United by the "actual people" has been overwhelming but ineffectual. There seems to be a general understanding in Congress that any legislation that they enact will again be ruled unconstitutional. This is indeed the probable outcome of any legislation. As such, many argue that the only possible solution to the problem – that the only way to once again remove corporate money from Congressional Elections – is to somehow propose and pass a specific Amendment to the Constitution pursuant to the Constitution's Article V, which will carves out a specific Constitutional exception which would allow Congress to exclude corporations from the political process without violating the [First Amendment]

Though much has been spoken and written about this possible option, no actual language for a proposed amendment had been brought forward, nor has any proposed Amendment gotten beyond Committee. In the end, the reality is that trying to write a statute or proposed Constitutional Provision to regulate any form of speech – political or otherwise – is both a dangerous process, and to coin an old phrase, a "slippery slope" that best not be stepped onto. So with a majority of the people viewing the situation as intolerable, the controversy lies adrift in a political paralysis of sorts, with no meaningful solution on the horizon.

There is a solution, and it is simple and immediate. This solution does not require enacting any new Federal Laws under the traditional law making process, only to have those laws challenged in Court and inevitably and eventually declared unconstitutional by the Supreme Court. The solution does not require proposing a Constitutional Amendment, a long and daunting process that is unlikely to ever get beyond the "talking phase" anyway. All that need be done is for Congress to police themselves. Or, to heal themselves: The effect of corporate money on the legislative process can immediately be excised simply by changing the Rules. Literally. The Rules of the Senate and the Rules of the House of Representatives. These Rules are beyond the reach of any Court, even the Supreme Court. While corporations may – according to the Supreme Court in their Citizen's United opinion – have [First Amendment] right to "political speech" equal to the "actual people", there is no corresponding right to purchase a Senator's or Representative's vote with unlimited direct or indirect financial campaign support or opposition. That a quid pro quo arrangement between a Member and a donor – corporate or "actual person" – is something that may without question be barred by law is a principle that no one would seriously dispute. In the modern legislative process, all substantive proposals and decisions are made and all meaningful votes taken in the various Committees and Sub-Committees during the writing and re-writing and revision process for proposed legislation.

There is no constitutional right of a Senator or Representative to participate in this Committee and Sub-Committee process at any level. It is solely the Rules of each House that define the Committee and Sub-Committee process, that define which Members and under what circumstances a Member may participate. And it is at this level of the legislation process that the support or opposition of a specific Member will make a difference to a corporation. By the time that legislation reaches the "Committee of the Whole" of each House in final form - ie. when the legislation is presented in final form to all 100 Members of the Senate and to all 435 voting Members of the House of Representatives - it is, practically speaking, too late for one or two members to change anything for their preferred corporate supporters. Certainly last minute changes can be made in the "Committee of the Whole" of either house, but such last minute changes can only be made in the House with the assent of hundreds of Members, and in the Senate with more than 50 Members. So, to solve the problem, all that need be done to remove the invidious impact of corporate money on the legislative process in Congress is to exclude - by RULE – any Member who has accepted corporate support. More importantly, no member or corporation can go to Court to challenge any of the RULES. There is nothing that they can do. What incentive does a corporation have to spend millions of dollars to support a candidate when that candidates will, by nature of the RULES, be prohibited in participating in the process at the only time that would matter to a corporation. The ills of Congress must be resolved through the political process. But to solve the ills of the Citizens United case and corporate money that it brings takes nothing more that the bona fide, real and genuine political will of the Members of Congress to do so. All Congress has to do is "CHANGE THE RULES". And then once again the Congress will be once again primarily concerned with the interests of "the people".

- Eugene Martin LaVergne

Third:

Equal Rights Amendment

First proposed in 1922, re-introduced in 1972, still NOT Ratified in 2016. 35 States have voted for Ratification, where the hell are the other 15?

Here's the entire text of the proposed Amendment:

'Section 1. _Equality of rights under the law shall not be denied or abridged by the United States or by any State on account of sex._

'Section 2. _The Congress shall have the power to enforce, by appropriate legislation, the provisions of this article._

'Section 3. _This article shall take effect 2 years after the date of ratification._'

This is not "Rocket Science" or "Brain Surgery", this is just common sense about human decency and dignity.

In 1922 this idea may have been radical, considering that the 19th Amendment giving women the Right to vote, had only been ratified on August 18th, 1920. Of course, women always had the "I have a headache" right to vote, but now it was official and the men in charge now get the headache.

Even Supreme Court Justice Ruth Bader Ginsburg agrees:
"If I could choose an amendment to add to the Constitution, it would be the Equal Rights Amendment,".

The ERA needs Ratification in only 3 more States or passage in the US Congress, Let's get this done and move on. The world moves whether we move or not, wouldn't you rather lead than follow?

It takes a very long time to change, but change for the better is a must and the country must continue to move forward and evolve or cease to exist as we know it. When we have a problem, we must strive to fix it, and if we get it wrong, must have the courage to try again.

It's taken the Supreme Court 226 years just to declare that *One* person, equals *One* person, and even then they equivocated and ruled that the States MAY use that standard for the Census and therefore used for District apportionment. We must change "MAY" into "SHALL" and truly have "*One* person equals *One* person", something even a 2 year-old intrinsically understands.

To make these and other things happen, "We the People" must have the power to influence our Representatives. We must go back to the "FIRST" step in the plan and make sure "ARTICLE THE FIRST" is followed and put into effect.

The "Pledge" will become much easier for our incoming Representatives, since most of the money will no longer be needed for year-long, multi-million dollar election campaigns. They will now be able to work during their 2 year terms and will be able to personally meet everyone in their district. A little shoe leather goes a long way.

The "Equal Rights Amendment", what more can I say:
In the words of that great Sage, "Larry the Cable Guy",
"Let's Get er Done!"

Fourth:

Not so fast, you're not getting away that easy. Just reading this outline and nodding isn't going to help. To save your Country and your Family, you're going to have to get your Ass out of that recliner and put forth some real effort and put a little "sweat equity" into the deal.

Here are some of the tools needed for this endeavor, We will get to the tools of last resort, (The ~~Second~~, now *Third* Amendment tools later). Information is everywhere, some good, some bad, and some totally misleading on purpose.

Go out and research the Equal Rights amendment. Research the Constitution and read about how we came to be the United States of America. Read, investigate, and then read some more. Unless you drop it on your foot, a book can't hurt you. It's been said that a "Little Knowledge" is dangerous, and that actually is true. Don't take Twitter, Facebook and Wikipedia as Gospel, jump in and get as much information as you can. It's as easy as "Hi Google" or "Hello Siri", and this you CAN do from your easy chair.

Here are a few of the tools that I recommend for the *ERA* and *"Article the First"*.

Thirty-Thousand.org (with the dash)

It will give you lots of Constitutional History related to "Article the First", and it will give you lots of background. Unfortunately, like every other book or resource published before October 2016, the conclusion was that "Article the First" was NOT ratified and that has now been found to be in error.

Yes, the history we have been taught for 200 years is wrong. What we have been taught and shown as the "Bill of Rights", the supposed first 10 Amendments, is wrong. Until now, most of the original documents, Bills and letters have either been missing, lost or destroyed, only available, if at all, in the Library of Congress, Libraries of various States and in private hands. Only now, with the advent of computer technology and digital imaging have these documents been sorted, viewed and consolidated to allow the story and the facts to emerge. They are now available in the new book:

"How *Less* is *More*: The Story of the *Real* First Amendment to the United States Constitution".
Written by Constitutional Scholar, Eugene Martin LaVergne
Edited and Published by me, Len Marshall, October 2016

Here's the short story behind the book with that long, long name. I call it the *"Hand Grenade on the Coffee Table"* because once it is read and understood, it's going to blow up the 2 political parties and turn Congress and Washington DC upside down. Facts are facts and the Law is the Law, with the Constitution being the Supreme Law of the Land and **"Article the First"** is the Law.

A few years back, Eugene being Eugene, began investigating the stories and history about "**ARTICLE THE FIRST**". His assumption was that it had never been Ratified and that it had never become part of the Constitution, just as we have all been taught. He wanted to document the story and put the rumors to rest permanently thereby removing any doubt about the Constitution and what we call the "Bill of Rights".

Midway thru his investigation, while literally crawling thru State archives, Eugene found the first documentation pointing to the Ratification of "**ARTICLE THE FIRST**". He called his brother, Fred and talked for hours. He then called me (by this time midnight) and we went on until 2 am. He was now fired up and going on a quest.

Six months go by and I get another call from Eugene. He wants to come to my house and show me some of the "stuff" that he has found. I had forgotten about it in the interim, but I told him to come on down. I figured that he had a box of Bills and old documents to show me, but instead shows up in a "Suburban" filled from the passenger side seat to the rear hatch, with books and documents in every condition imagineable. He starts unloading the truck in my front room and office which have now become impassable and in the next breath mentions that he writing a book, would I help? And that was the start.

2 years, 10s of thousands of documents, 3000+ photos taken, (1000 or so used in the book itself) hundreds of books and thousands of online searches later, we now have a book that I can personally certify and vouch for.

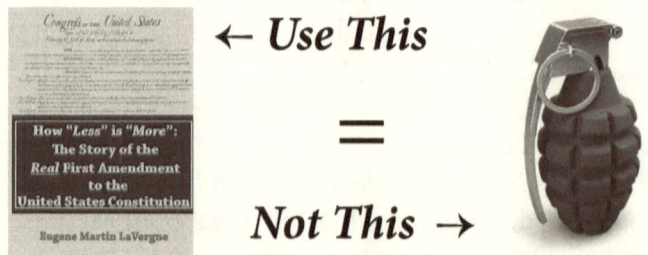

It is available on CreateSpace and Amazon in book form: ISBN: 978-0998299303 and in Kindle form, ASIN: B01N69X1YZ

The next tool in the box is for the ERA.
Read and investigate everywhere, educate yourself and make your own decisions, but at least go to the Source:
EQUALRIGHTSAMENDMENT.ORG

IF WE CAN ACCOMPLISH THESE GOALS, WE WILL BE WELL ON OUR WAY TO MAKING OUR COUNTRY THE BEST IT HAS EVER BEEN, THE BEST THE WORLD HAS EVER SEEN.
- LEN MARSHALL

THIS OUTLINE IS ABOUT IDEAS IN THE POLITICAL ARENA. IT IS NOT PARTISAN, NEITHER LEFT NOR RIGHT, PROGRESSIVE OR CONSERVATIVE. GOOD AND BAD IDEAS ARE JUST THAT, NOT DEMOCRAT OR REPUBLICAN, JUST GOOD OR BAD.

If things go really bad we might have to revert to 2nd amendment remedies and gold and silver for money. I don't know about you, but I can't afford gold, I did buy some silver once, tore right thru my pocket and rolled down the street. And I'm totally against concealed carry. The last time I did that, my Mossberg 500 tore up my leg.

WE HAVE TO KEEP THINGS FROM GETTING THAT BAD, I DOUBT THAT I WOULD SURVIVE AND THEN WHO WOULD BE THERE TO PROTECT MY FAMILY AND COUNTRY? WILL YOU?

I HAVE ANOTHER QUESTION FOR YOU.
WHY CAN OUR OFFICIALS AND CANDIDATES LIE TO US, BUT IT'S ILLEGAL FOR US TO LIE TO OFFICIALS?

Now comes the big test that I was hinting at. Could you pass the Naturalization test and become a US Citizen?
Even more importantly:
What happens to a US Citizen who *fails* this test? (See last page).

The 97 civics (history and government) questions and answers for the naturalization test are listed below. The civics test is an oral test and the USCIS Officer will ask the applicant up to 10 of the 97 civics questions.

An applicant must answer 6 out of 10 questions correctly to pass the civics portion of the naturalization test.

On the naturalization test, some answers may change because of elections or appointments. As you study for the test, make sure that you know the most current answers to these questions. Answer these questions with the name of the official who is serving at the time of your eligibility interview with USCIS. The USCIS Officer will not accept an incorrect answer.

Although USCIS is aware that there may be additional correct answers to the 97 civics questions, applicants are encouraged to respond to the civics questions using the answers provided below. The actual test itself is mostly multiple choice with changes due to location and date.

I am not providing the answers for you, look them up yourself.

AMERICAN GOVERNMENT
A: Principles of American Democracy

1. What is the supreme law of the land?
2. What does the Constitution do?
3. The idea of self-government is in the first three words of the Constitution. What are these words?
4. What is an amendment?
5. What do we call the first ten amendments to the Constitution?
6. What is one right or freedom from the First Amendment?
7. How many amendments does the Constitution have?
8. What did the Declaration of Independence do?
9. What are two rights in the Declaration of Independence?
10. What is freedom of religion?
11. What is the economic system in the United States?

12. What is the "rule of law"?

13. Name one branch or part of the government.

14. What stops one branch of government from becoming too powerful?

15. Who is in charge of the executive branch?

16. Who makes federal laws?

17. What are the two parts of the U.S. Congress?

18. How many U.S. Senators are there?

19. We elect a U.S. Senator for how many years?

20. Who is one of your state's U.S. Senators now?

21. The House of Representatives has how many voting members?

22. We elect a U.S. Representative for how many years?

23. Name your U.S. Representative.

24. Who does a U.S. Senator represent?

25. Why do some states have more Representatives than other states?

26. We elect a President for how many years?

27. In what month do we vote for President?

28. What is the name of the President of the United States now?

29. What is the name of the Vice President of the United States now?

30. If the President can no longer serve, who becomes President?

31. If both the President and the Vice President can no longer serve, who becomes President?

32. Who is the Commander in Chief of the military?

33. Who signs bills to become laws?

34. Who vetoes bills?

35. What does the President's Cabinet do?

36. What are two Cabinet-level positions?

37. What does the judicial branch do?

38. What is the highest court in the United States?

39. How many justices are on the Supreme Court?

40. Who is the Chief Justice of the United States now?

41. Under our Constitution, some powers belong to the federal government. What is one power of the federal government?

42. Under our Constitution, some powers belong to the states. What is one power of the states?

43. Who is the Governor of your state now?

44. What is the capital of your state?

45. What are the two major political parties in the United States?

46. What is the political party of the President now?

47. What is the name of the Speaker of the House of Representatives now?

48. There are four amendments to the Constitution about who can vote. Describe one of them.

49. What is one responsibility that is only for United States citizens?

50. Name one right only for United States citizens.

51. What are two rights of everyone living in the United States?

52. What do we show loyalty to when we say the Pledge of Allegiance?

53. What is one promise you make when you become a United States citizen?

54. How old do citizens have to be to vote for President?

55. What are two ways that Americans can participate in their democracy?

56. When is the last day you can send in federal income tax forms?

57. When must all men register for the Selective Service?

58. What is one reason colonists came to America?

59. Who lived in America before the Europeans arrived?

60. What group of people was taken to America and sold as slaves?

61. Why did the colonists fight the British?

62. Who wrote the Declaration of Independence?

63. When was the Declaration of Independence adopted?

64. There were 13 original states. Name three.

65. What happened at the Constitutional Convention?

66. When was the Constitution written?

67. The Federalist Papers supported the passage of the U.S. Constitution. Name one of the writers.

68. What is one thing Benjamin Franklin is famous for?

69. Who is the "Father of Our Country"?

70. Who was the first President?

71. What territory did the United States buy from France in 1803?

72. Name one war fought by the United States in the 1800s.

73. Name the U.S. war between the North and the South.

74. Name one problem that led to the Civil War.

75. What was one important thing that Abraham Lincoln did?

76. What did the Emancipation Proclamation do?

77. What did Susan B. Anthony do?

78. Name one war fought by the United States in the 1900s.

79. Who was President during World War I?

80. Who was President during the Great Depression and World War II?

81. Who did the United States fight in World War II?

82. Before he was President, Eisenhower was a general. What war was he in?

83. During the Cold War, what was the main concern of the United States?

84. What movement tried to end racial discrimination?

85. What did Martin Luther King, Jr. do?

86. What major event happened on September 11, 2001, in the United States?

87. Name one American Indian tribe in the United States.

INTEGRATED CIVICS
A: Geography

88. Name one of the two longest rivers in the United States.

89. What ocean is on the West Coast of the United States?

90. What ocean is on the East Coast of the United States?

91. Name one U.S. territory.

92. Name one state that borders Canada.

93. Name one state that borders Mexico.

94. What is the capital of the United States?

95. Where is the Statue of Liberty?

96. Why does the flag have 13 stripes?

97. Why does the flag have 50 stars?

Information supplied by: www.uscis.gov

Here is a breakdown of Allowed national
and state government powers:

* Print money
* Regulate interstate (between states) and international trade
* Make treaties and conduct foreign policy
* Declare war
* Provide an army and navy
* Establish post offices
* Make laws necessary and proper to carry out the these powers
* Issue licenses
* Regulate intrastate (within the state) businesses
* Conduct elections
* Establish local governments
* Ratify amendments to the Constitution
* Take measures for public health and safety
* May exert powers the Constitution does not delegate to the national government or prohibit the states from using.

In addition to their exclusive powers, both the national government and state governments
share the power of being able to:

* Collect taxes
* Build roads
* Borrow money
* Establish courts
* Make and enforce laws
* Charter banks and corporations
* Spend money for the general welfare
* Take private property for public purposes, with just compensation

Source: The U.S. Government Printing Office

Powers Denied the Government

What the national and state governments are *Not* allowed to do in the United States.

* May not violate the Bill of Rights
* May not impose export taxes among states
* May not use money from the Treasury without the passage and approval of an appropriations bill
* May not change state boundaries
* May not enter into treaties with other countries
* May not print money
* May not tax imports or exports
* May not impair obligations of contracts
* May not suspend a person's rights without due process

In addition, *neither* the national government nor state governments may:

* Grant titles of nobility
* Permit slavery (13th Amendment)
* Deny citizens the right to vote due to race, color, or previous servitude (15th Amendment)
* Deny citizens the right to vote because of gender (19th Amendment)

Source: The U.S. Government Printing Office

<u>*Nothing !*</u>

And that's a big problem. Of course, US Citizens don't have to take this test, only non-citizens wanting to become US Citizens need to study and learn these basic facts about our Country. And that's the root of the problem. US Citizens have to do *Nothing* to become or stay US Citizens, in fact, it's almost impossible to lose your Natural-born citizenship, in sharp contrast with a Naturalized Citizens rights.

Uninformed, misinformed, misled, uneducated, indoctrinated, unemployed or underemployed citizens are the greatest threat to our country's survival. Don't worry about Iran, Radical Islam, Noth Korea, China or Russia. Don't worry about Climate change or Global warming, the biggest threat is right here, walking among us.

If you see a problem, try and fix it, if you can't, find someone or something that can help. If you don't like something, if it's appropriate, say something. Discuss your ideas, even if you are wrong, you will learn from the experience. Get the facts, and once you have found you are correct, teach others. Teach your sons and daughters, spread the information thru friends and family, that's all you need to do. Imagine what would happen if we each sat down with our families and friends and discussed the "Golden Rule", or picked any one of the "Ten Commandments" and talked about it. Discuss how to make a better life for yourself and your circle of influence. Encourage discerning education, learn and then teach how to harvest facts and truth from the trash that is thrown at us every day.

Do this every day, not just on a Friday, Saturday or Sunday, make it a habit and you will find you are a better human being for it, and almost by accident, a better citizen.

And a better citizen is what is needed to save our Country, our Family and our collective butts.